THE COMPLETE POKER HANDBOOK

A Guide for Players of All Skill-levels
Composed By Jeremy B. Keefer

This Poker Handbook Belongs To:_____.

www.trafford.com

North America & international
toll-free: 1 888 232 4444 (USA & Canada)
phone: 250 383 6864 ◆ fax: 812 355 4082

Table of Contents

Foreword

Over the past decade, poker has become one of the most popular games around the world. Its popularity soars for a variety of reasons: many life lessons can be learned from playing; it's a great way to meet new people; it's enjoyable; and most importantly, when skill and luck are combined, players can make a ton of money playing the game. Also, in poker, there are no barriers—race, gender, physical handicaps, and other differences are overlooked while battling on the green felt.

I am fortunate to have started playing poker at a relatively early stage in my life. Although I am certainly not the best poker player in the world, I work to improve my game each week. The game has taught me a great deal about life, including how to deal with situations and how important it is to manage income and costs. Also, I've made some great friends as a result of playing poker.

Whether you are a beginner at this great game or a seasoned professional, this handbook will help you to keep a record of your performance, maintain an edge over key opponents, learn from memorable hands and various situations, and discover aspects about your own game that you never realized before. Devise some strategies for tournament play or ring games, write them down in the Strategies section, and implement them into your play. Experiment a little and keep a record of everything you do at the poker table, learning from your successes and failures. As most successful players will tell you, keeping detailed records about every aspect of your game is a key step toward success.

Whatever it is you wish to accomplish in the poker world, I wish you well and good luck at the tables!

Jeremy Keefer

My Strategies

My Strategies

My Strategies

_____

_____

_____

_____

_____

_____

_____

_____

_____

_____

_____

_____

_____

_____

_____

_____

_____

Earnings Chart

How to use this earnings chart:

Following a session, enter the date of the session in the "Date" column.

Following the date, write in the location and game type (tournament or cash game). Then, enter the number of hours played during the session.

In the "Earnings" category, enter your profit or loss for the specific session. For example, if the buy-in was $120 and you cashed out $600, your earnings for the session would be $480.

To calculate your Earnings Per Hour, simply divide your total profit for the session by the number of hours you played.

To calculate your Career Earnings, simply add the session earnings (or subtract your losses) with your career earnings total from the line above. A sample chart is included below to demonstrate this:

Earnings Chart						
Date	Location	Game Type	Hrs	Earnings (Losses)	Earnings Per Hour	Career Earnings
1/1/09	Harrahs	Tourn	5.5	$1245	$226.36	$1245
1/3/09	John's	Cash	4	$340	$85	$1585
1/7/09	Harrahs	Cash	3	-$300	-$100	$1285
2/1/09	FullTilt	Tourn	7	$984	$140.57	$2269
2/4/09	John's	Cash	6.5	$232	$37.12	$2501
2/7/09	Harrahs	Cash	2	-$240	-$120	$2261
2/9/09	Harrahs	Tourn	4.5	$352	$74.11	$2613

Earnings Chart						
Date	Location	Game Type	Hours	Earnings (Losses)	Earnings Per Hour	Career Earnings

Earnings Chart						
Date	Location	Game Type	Hours	Earnings (Losses)	Earnings Per Hour	Career Earnings

Earnings Chart						
Date	Location	Game Type	Hours	Earnings (Losses)	Earnings Per Hour	Career Earnings

Earnings Chart						
Date	Location	Game Type	Hours	Earnings (Losses)	Earnings Per Hour	Career Earnings

Earnings Chart						
Date	Location	Game Type	Hours	Earnings (Losses)	Earnings Per Hour	Career Earnings

Earnings Chart						
Date	Location	Game Type	Hours	Earnings (Losses)	Earnings Per Hour	Career Earnings

Earnings Chart						
Date	Location	Game Type	Hours	Earnings (Losses)	Earnings Per Hour	Career Earnings

Earnings Chart						
Date	Location	Game Type	Hours	Earnings (Losses)	Earnings Per Hour	Career Earnings

Earnings Chart						
Date	Location	Game Type	Hours	Earnings (Losses)	Earnings Per Hour	Career Earnings

Earnings Chart						
Date	Location	Game Type	Hours	Earnings (Losses)	Earnings Per Hour	Career Earnings

			Earnings Chart			
Date	Location	Game Type	Hours	Earnings (Losses)	Earnings Per Hour	Career Earnings

Earnings Chart						
Date	Location	Game Type	Hours	Earnings (Losses)	Earnings Per Hour	Career Earnings

Earnings Chart						
Date	Location	Game Type	Hours	Earnings (Losses)	Earnings Per Hour	Career Earnings

Earnings Chart						
Date	Location	Game Type	Hours	Earnings (Losses)	Earnings Per Hour	Career Earnings

Earnings Chart						
Date	Location	Game Type	Hours	Earnings (Losses)	Earnings Per Hour	Career Earnings

Earnings Chart						
Date	Location	Game Type	Hours	Earnings (Losses)	Earnings Per Hour	Career Earnings

Earnings Chart						
Date	Location	Game Type	Hours	Earnings (Losses)	Earnings Per Hour	Career Earnings

Earnings Chart						
Date	Location	Game Type	Hours	Earnings (Losses)	Earnings Per Hour	Career Earnings

Earnings Chart						
Date	Location	Game Type	Hours	Earnings (Losses)	Earnings Per Hour	Career Earnings

Earnings Chart						
Date	Location	Game Type	Hours	Earnings (Losses)	Earnings Per Hour	Career Earnings

Earnings Chart						
Date	Location	Game Type	Hours	Earnings (Losses)	Earnings Per Hour	Career Earnings

Earnings Chart						
Date	Location	Game Type	Hours	Earnings (Losses)	Earnings Per Hour	Career Earnings

Player Notes

Name:_____ Style:_____

Tells:_____

_____

_____

Strengths:_____

_____

_____

Weaknesses:_____

_____

_____

Notes:_____

_____

_____

_____

_____

_____

_____

_____

_____

Player Notes

Name:_____   Style:_____

Tells:_____

_____

_____

Strengths:_____

_____

_____

Weaknesses:_____

_____

_____

Notes:_____

_____

_____

_____

_____

_____

_____

_____

Player Notes

Name:_____   Style:_____

Tells:_____

_____

_____

Strengths:_____

_____

_____

Weaknesses:_____

_____

_____

Notes:_____

_____

_____

_____

_____

_____

_____

_____

Player Notes

Name:_____   Style:_____

Tells:_____

_____

_____

Strengths:_____

_____

_____

Weaknesses:_____

_____

_____

Notes:_____

_____

_____

_____

_____

_____

_____

_____

_____

Player Notes

Name:_____   Style:_____

Tells:_____

_____

_____

Strengths:_____

_____

_____

Weaknesses:_____

_____

_____

Notes:_____

_____

_____

_____

_____

_____

_____

_____

Player Notes

Name:_____   Style:_____

Tells:_____

_____

_____

Strengths:_____

_____

_____

Weaknesses:_____

_____

_____

Notes:_____

_____

_____

_____

_____

_____

_____

Player Notes

Name:_____   Style:_____

Tells:_____

_____

_____

Strengths:_____

_____

_____

Weaknesses:_____

_____

_____

Notes:_____

_____

_____

_____

_____

_____

_____

_____

Player Notes

Name:_____   Style:_____

Tells:_____

_____

_____

Strengths:_____

_____

_____

Weaknesses:_____

_____

_____

Notes:_____

_____

_____

_____

_____

_____

_____

_____

_____

Player Notes

Name:_____   Style:_____

Tells:_____

_____

_____

Strengths:_____

_____

_____

Weaknesses:_____

_____

_____

Notes:_____

_____

_____

_____

_____

_____

_____

_____

_____

Player Notes

Name:_____   Style:_____

Tells:_____

_____

_____

Strengths:_____

_____

_____

Weaknesses:_____

_____

_____

Notes:_____

_____

_____

_____

_____

_____

_____

_____

_____

Player Notes

Name:_____   Style:_____

Tells:_____

_____

_____

Strengths:_____

_____

_____

Weaknesses:_____

_____

_____

Notes:_____

_____

_____

_____

_____

_____

_____

_____

Player Notes

Name:_____   Style:_____

Tells:_____

_____

_____

Strengths:_____

_____

_____

Weaknesses:_____

_____

_____

Notes:_____

_____

_____

_____

_____

_____

_____

_____

Player Notes

Name:_____   Style:_____

Tells:_____

_____

_____

Strengths:_____

_____

_____

Weaknesses:_____

_____

_____

Notes:_____

_____

_____

_____

_____

_____

_____

_____

Player Notes

Name:_____   Style:_____

Tells:_____

_____

_____

Strengths:_____

_____

_____

Weaknesses:_____

_____

_____

Notes:_____

_____

_____

_____

_____

_____

_____

_____

_____

Personal Notes

Personal Notes

Personal Notes

Memorable Hands

_____

_____

_____

_____

_____

_____

_____

_____

_____

_____

_____

Memorable Hands

65

Memorable Hands

Memorable Hands

_____

_____

_____

_____

_____

_____

_____

_____

_____

_____

_____

Memorable Hands

_____

_____

_____

_____

_____

_____

_____

_____

_____

_____

_____

Memorable Hands

_____

_____

_____

_____

_____

_____

_____

_____

_____

_____

Memorable Hands

Memorable Hands

Memorable Hands

Memorable Hands

Glossary of Poker Terms

A-Game – when one is playing to the best of his ability

ABC Player – a predictable player who typically plays the same types of hands and utilizes the same betting patterns

Ace High – a hand in which a player has no pair and an Ace is his highest valued card

Ace in the Hole – when one hole card is an Ace

Ace-to-Five – the lowest straight possible (A-2-3-4-5); also called the "Wheel" or the "Bicycle"

Aces Full – a full house consisting of three Aces and another pair

Aces Up – a pair of Aces along with a second pair (for example: A-A-3-3)

Act – occurs when a player checks, calls, raises, or folds

Action – checking, betting, raising, or re-raising; a game with a lot of loose players

Add-On – an option available in some tournaments which allows a player to "buy" additional chips to add to his stack, usually at the end of the re-buy period

Advantage – *see Edge*

Advertise – to make it appear as though you have a strong or weak hand (for example: if you have a strong hand and wish to get drawing hands out of the pot, you may want to demonstrate a strong hand to force a fold; if you hold the nuts, you may want to demonstrate that you have a weaker hand than your opponent or a drawing hand to induce a call or raise)

Aggressive – a player who bets heavily on draws and made hands

Ahead – in terms of betting position, if Player 1 acts before Player 2, Player 1 acts "ahead" of Player 2; in terms of hands, the player who is "ahead" currently has the best hand

Ajax – when a player's hole cards are an Ace and a Jack

All-in – when a player commits all of his chips to the pot

Ammunition, Ammo – refers to chips in one's stack

Announced Bet – a verbal bet (for example: if a player wishes to bet $50, he can verbally state that the bet is $50 before placing the chips in the pot)

Ante – a bet that is required by all players at the table before each deal (antes ensure there is money in the pot before players get their cards)

Automatic – refers to a situation in which a player must bet

Backdoor Flush Draw – a drawing hand in which a player has three suited cards and needs one more of the same suit on the turn and another on the river to make a flush

Backdoor Straight Draw – a drawing hand in which a player has three cards for a straight and needs cards on the turn and the river to make a straight

Backer – someone who finances a poker player

Bad Beat – occurs when a player with a much better hand gets beat by a weaker hand

Bad Beat Jackpot – a sum of money that is divided up amongst the players at the table when one player incurs a bad beat; jackpot amounts and rules vary from house to house

Bankroll – the funds a poker player has available to play with

Barn – slang for "Full House"

Battle of the Blinds – occurs when all players fold except for the ones who have posted the blinds

Behind – in terms of betting position, if Player 1 acts before Player 2 in the hand, Player 2 is "behind" Player 1; in terms of hands, "behind" refers to the hand that is currently weaker than another player's hand

Belly-Buster – *see Inside Straight-Draw*

Bet – placing chips into the pot after a new card is dealt

Bet in the Dark – a bet made by a player before he sees the next card(s)

Bet Into – occurs when one player makes the initial bet in a round of betting and another player makes the initial bet in the next betting round

Bet the Limit – in limit games, the maximum bet allowed

Bet the Pot – a bet that equals the amount that is already in the pot

Big Blind – the second player to the left of the current dealer; this player must post a pre-determined amount ensuring there is money in the pot before the hand is dealt

Big Hand – a strong hand

Big Pair – a pair of 10s, Jacks, Queens, Kings, or Aces

Big Slick – when a player holds one ace and one king as his/her hole cards

Blank – a card that does not improve any of the players' hands

Blind Bet – to bet prior to looking at one's hand or the next card

Blind Robber – someone who raises before the flop and wins the blinds

Blinds – bets that the two players to the left of the dealer are required to post prior to any hands being dealt

Bluff – a bet by a player with a weak hand to get all others to fold their hands

Board –the cards that are used by all players in the hand; also called "community cards"

Boat – *see Full House*

Bottom Pair – occurs when a player pairs the lowest card on the board

Bring-In – a forced bet in stud games on the first round of betting

Broadway – a straight from ten to ace (10-J-Q-K-A)

Bubble – in tournaments, the "bubble" refers to the highest place finish that pays no money (for example: in a tournament that pays the top ten finishers, the player who finishes eleventh is said to "finish on the bubble" because he/she is the last player to be eliminated and win no money)

Bullets – pocket Aces

Burn Card – a card that is not used which is dealt facedown prior to dealing a round of cards

Bury Card – a card that is taken from the top of the deck and placed in the middle

Bust Out – to be eliminated from a tournament by losing all of one's chips

Busted Hand – a drawing hand that failed to hit

Button – the player who acts as the dealer in the current hand; *also see Dealer Button*

"Buy the Pot" – refers to a situation where a player bets and all others fold

Buy-in – the amount a player spends to get into a game

C-Note – a one-hundred dollar bill

Call – to match an opponent's bet or raise and continue with the hand

Caller – one who makes a call

Calling Station – a player that makes a lot of calls, even with possibilities of having a losing hand

Cap – to make the last allowable bet in a hand

Case Card – the final card of a particular value in the deck (for example: if one player holds a Q and two other players each folded a Q, there is only one Q left in the deck to come out—the case Queen)

Cash Out – to leave a ring game and exchange your chips for cash

Catch – occurs when a player hits a card that improves his/her hand

Center Pot – *see Main Pot*

Change Gears – refers to a player changing his/her style of play or betting patterns in order to deceive opponents or to "change his/her luck"

Chase – occurs when a player has a drawing hand and is "chasing" one or more cards to make a hand

Check – if no bet was made ahead of a player, he/she has the option to stay in the hand without committing any more chips to the pot

Check-Call – occurs when Player 1 checks his/her hand, Player 2 bets, and Player 1 calls the bet

Check-Fold – occurs when Player 1 checks his/her hand, Player 2 bets, and Player 1 folds the hand

Check-Raise – occurs when Player 1 checks his/her hand, Player 2 bets, and Player 1 raises the bet by Player 2

Chips – round disks that symbolize money in the poker world

Chop – the term used to describe two or more players evenly splitting a pot

Clean Out – a card that would almost guarantee that one's hand is best (for example: if a player holds 6-8 and the board is 7-6-9-2, a 10 would be a clean out because it would likely give him the best hand—only one other hand would win in that situation: J-8)

Cold Call – to call multiple bets, even when no chips were previously invested into the pot

Cold Deck – a deck from which many weak hands are currently being dealt; a deck of cards that has been fixed by a cheater

Cold Hands – refers to a string of hands in which a player receives weak cards

Community Cards – the cards that are dealt face-up and used by all players in the hand

Complete Hand – a hand that is defined by all five cards (straight, flush, full house, four-of-a-kind, or straight flush)

Connectors – two or more cards in sequence (for example: 8-9)

Conservative Play – only playing premium hands that have little risk

Counterfeit – a player is "counterfeited" when he/she has the best hand at one point, but loses the hand because of a card (or cards) that come out (for example: if Player 1 has 9-9 and Player 2 has Q-J, and the board is Q-6-9-6, Player 1 would be counterfeited if another Q hits the river— Nines-full-of-sixes would be beaten by Queens-full-of-sixes)

Cowboys – pocket Kings

Crack – to beat a better hand, usually a big pocket pair such as aces or kings

Cripple – to seriously ruin one's chances in a tournament by taking most of his chips; to "cripple the deck" means that a player has most or all of the cards that one would want with the current board

Crying Call – a reluctant call of a bet

Cut Card – a card that is placed at the bottom of the deck so players at the table cannot see the bottom card of the deck

Cut the Deck – to divide the deck prior to the deal, therefore placing different cards at the top

Dead Man's Hand – one Ace and one eight

Dead Money – chips that are committed to the pot because a player bet out of turn; also used to describe a weak player who has little chance of making money in the game

Deal – occurs when the dealer gives each player his/her cards

"Deal Me In" – a request by a player who has gotten up from the table to be dealt cards

"Deal Me Out" – a request by a player who wishes not to receive cards for the current hand

Dealer – the person who shuffles and deals the cards and monitors the table

Dealer Button – a marker, usually a white disk, that is used to show which player at the table would be the current dealer

Dealer's Choice – a poker game in which the person dealing the cards can name which type of poker game is to be played for the current hand

Deck – a set of cards (typically 52) used to play poker

Deuces – a pair of twos

Dog – slang for "Underdog"

Dominated Hand – a hand that is weaker than another hand, typically because one card is the same as the opponent's but the other is lower in value (a hand in which the kicker is lower than the opponent's)

Donkey – refers to a player who makes unwise decisions

Door Card – the first face-up card in stud games

Double Belly-Buster – a straight draw in which the player needs one of two "inside" cards to make a straight (for example: 6-8-9-10-Q; in this case, the player can hit either a 7 or a J to make a straight); also called a "double gutshot straight draw)

Double Up – occurs when a player goes all-in, is called, and wins, therefore doubling his/her chip count

Down-and-Dirty – the final cards that are dealt in a seven-card stud game; known as down and dirty because they are dealt facedown

Down Cards – cards that are dealt facedown; also known as "hole cards"

Draw – occurs when a player has outs that would make his/her hand much better; in draw games, this occurs when players discard cards they don't wish to keep and are dealt new ones

Draw Card – in draw games, a card that a player receives after discarding cards he/she does not wish to keep

Draw for Seats – each player chooses a card from a facedown deck to determine where he/she will sit for the game

Draw Game – a type of poker game where players are dealt cards, can discard some of them, and receive new cards in their place to make a hand

Drawing Dead – occurs when a player cannot hit any remaining card to win the hand

Drawing Hand – a hand in which the player is looking to hit a certain card(s) to make the hand much stronger; the player is usually looking for a card to make a straight or a flush

Drawing Thin – when a player is drawing to just one or a few outs

Driver's Seat – a player who is said to be "in the driver's seat" is one who is making a lot of initial bets

Ducks – a pair of twos

Early Position – one of the first few people to act in the hand; these players have a disadvantage because they cannot see the other players' actions before they act

Edge – an advantage (usually based on position or skill level)

Edge Odds – the advantage or disadvantage of a player relative to all other players in the hand

Elimination – occurs when a player goes all-in and loses, thus getting knocked out of the game; typically refers to tournament play since the player cannot typically buy in again

End Bet – the last bet of a round

Entry Fee – a fee that is paid to the house to enter a tournament

Equity – a player's rightful share of a pot

Even Money – a bet made in hopes of winning the wagered amount from one's opponent

Exposed Card – a card that is unintentionally flipped face-up

Extra Blind – a blind posted by a player who is entering or returning to a table, or for changing his position at the table

Face Card – a king, queen, or jack; called face cards because they have "faces" on them

False Cut – a form of cheating in which the dealer makes the appearance of cutting the deck, while the same cards remain at the top

Family Pot – a hand in which all or most of the players at the table remain in the hand

Fast Play – aggressive play that includes a lot of betting and raising

Favorite – the player with the best odds of winning a hand

Fifth Street – in hold'em and omaha, the final community card to be dealt; in seven-card stud, the third face-up card in each player's hand

Fill Up – to make a full house (for example: if a player has A-9 and the board is A-Q-5-9, he will "fill up" with an A or 9 on the river for a full house)

Fish – a weak player who typically loses money

Fishhooks – pocket Jacks

Five-Card Draw – a poker game in which each player is dealt five cards face-down and has one draw to replace particular cards to make the best hand

Five-Card Stud – a poker game in which each player is dealt one face-down card and four face-up cards with betting rounds taking place after each up-card is dealt

Fixed Limit – a variation of poker in which there is a limit to what players can bet

Flat Call – to simply call a bet with a strong hand, rather than raise

Flat Limit – a version of fixed-limit poker in which all bets are the same amount

Floorperson – a cardroom supervisor who understands the rules and settles disputes

Flop – in hold'em and Omaha, the first three community cards that are dealt simultaneously

Flush – a hand in which a player has 5 cards of the same suit

Flush Draw – a hand in which a player needs a card(s) to make a flush

Fold – an action in which a player mucks his/her cards and does not commit any more of his/her chips to the pot, therefore getting out of the hand

Fold Equity – added value a player receives when he gets an opponent to fold rather than call and showdown

Forced Bet – a required bet that starts the action on the first round of a hand

Four-of-a-Kind – occurs when a player has four of the same card (for example: 6-6-6-6)

Fourth Street – in hold'em and Omaha, the fourth community card that is dealt face-up; in seven-card stud and razz, the second face-up card dealt to each player in the hand

Free Card – when all players in the hand check during a round, thus everyone sees the next card "for free"

Freeroll – a tournament in which players can join for free

Freeze-Out – a game that pursues until one player has all the money

Full Boat – *see Full House*

Full House – a hand in which a player has three of one card and two of another (for example: A-A-A-9-9)

Gap Hand – a hand in which the hole cards are not the same value or connectors (there is a gap between cards, such as 3-9)

"Get Full Value" – with the best hand, betting or raising the maximum amount that your opponent will call

"Go All-In" – to risk all of one's chips on a hand

Gravy – winnings

Grind – playing conservatively and earning modest returns over a long period of time

Gutshot – *see Inside Straight Draw*

Gutshot Straight Draw – *see Inside Straight Draw*

Hand – one's best five cards

Heads Up – a game or hand in which only two players are playing

Head-to-Head – *see Heads Up*

High Card – in a hand where no player has a pair or better, the player with the card of highest value wins the pot

High Hand – the best hand in a round of poker

High Limit – a game in which the stakes are high

High-Low – games in which both the highest and the lowest hands each earn a share of the pot

High-Low Split – *see High-Low*

High Roller – a player with a large bankroll who typically plays high stakes games

Hit – to catch a card (or cards) to improve a hand

Hit-and-Run – entering a ring game, winning big, and cashing out in a short period of time

Hold'em – a version of poker in which each player makes his/her hand by using the best five-card combination from two hole cards and five community cards

Hole Cards – the cards that are dealt facedown to an individual player that are only used by that respective player

Home Game – a game held amongst friends, rather than a game held at a casino or cardroom

Hook – a Jack

Hot Deck – a deck that has recently dealt many strong hands

Hot Hands – a streak of high-valued hands

Hot Seat – a seat at a poker table in which players have received many winning hands

House – the host of a card game; usually, the house will take a portion of each pot or an entry fee to pay for hosting the game

House Rules – any rules that are adopted by the place where poker is being played

Implied Odds – calling or betting with the assumption that the next card(s) to come will win the hand

Improve – to hit cards to strengthen one's hand

Inside Straight Draw – a straight draw in which a player can hit only one card to make a straight (for example: if a player has 7-8 in the hole and the board is 4-5-A, he/she needs a 6 to make a straight)

Isolate – to bet, getting most of the players out of the hand, thus giving the bettor greater odds of winning the pot

Jackpot – *see Bad Beat Jackpot*

Jam – a hand in which many players are raising

Key Card – a card that gives a player a big draw or completes his hand

Kicker – when two or more players have one of the same card, the kickers are the other hole cards, which typically determine who wins the pot (for example: say player 1 has A-6 in his hand and player 2 has A-10; the 6 is player 1's kicker while the 10 is player 2's kicker; since the 10 is higher than the 6, player two would have a better hand)

Knock-Out – to eliminate a player from a tournament

Ladies – pocket Queens

Late Position – refers to the player on the dealer button and the player to the dealer's right; these players have late position because most of the other players act before them; late position is typically favorable because those players get to see how the others act before it is their turn

Lay Down – to fold

Leak – a weakness in one's game that causes the player to lose money

Limit – the maximum amount that can be bet or raised at any one time

Limit Poker – any type of poker game in which there is a maximum betting structure per round of betting

Limp – *see Limp In*

Limper – one who usually just calls the big blind, rather than raising or folding; limpers typically see a lot of flops, especially in tighter games

Limp In – the term used to describe when a player simply calls the big blind, rather than raising it or folding

Little Blind – *see Small Blind*

Live Blind – a blind with the option to raise

Live Cards – when a player has lower cards than his opponent, they are said to be "live" if the opponent does not hold any of the same card (for example: Player 1 holds A-9 while Player 2 holds 9-10—Player 2 does not hold live cards because if the 9 hits he still has the second-best hand; If Player 1 holds A-9 and Player 2 holds 10-J, Player 2 does have live cards because he can hit either of his hole cards to make a winning hand)

Lock-Up – when a player is joining a game and has his seat reserved

Loose – a style of play in which a player plays a lot of hands and sees a lot of flops

Loose Game – a game with many loose players

Low Limit – a poker game in which the bet sizes are small

Low Card – the lowest up-card in seven-card stud games, which is required to bet

Luck – an aspect of poker in which some people believe, that brings good fortune to poker players

Luck-Out – to outdraw an opponent who had a better hand

Made Hand – a hand that is complete (for example: a straight)

Main Pot – when a short-stacked player is all-in and betting continues afterward, the main pot is what the short-stacked player can win if he makes the best hand; it consists of the chips wagered by the short-stack along with matching chips by all others who remain in the hand

Make a Hand – occurs when a player hits a card or cards to make a complete hand (such as a straight or a flush)

Marked Cards – cards that have been altered so a player will know what they are while the other players will not; marking cards is a form of cheating and therefore is illegal

Maximum Buy-In – the highest cash amount a player can use to buy-in to a particular game

Mechanic – someone who cheats by rigging the deck and dealing strong hands to certain players

Micro-Limit – poker games with very small stakes, such as $.02/$.04 blinds

Middle Pair – occurs when a player uses one of his hole cards to make a pair with the middle-valued card showing on the flop

Middle Position – the middle third of players to act in a hand

Minimum Buy-In – the lowest cash amount a player can use to buy-in to a particular game

Min-Pop – a raise that is double that of the original bet

Misdeal – a mistake made while dealing, which results in a re-deal

Miss – not completing a drawing hand when all the cards are dealt

Missed Blind – a required bet that is posted by a player who was away from the table while he was supposed to be big or small blind

Monster- a very strong hand

Muck – to throw away a hand facedown and forfeit the pot

Muck Pile – a collection of folded hands that are no longer in play

No-Limit – in no-limit poker games, there are no restrictions to the size of a bet except that it must be greater than or equal to the big blind amount

No-Limit Hold'em – a version of hold'em in which players can raise any amount greater than or equal to the big blind; a player can go all-in at any time in the game when it is his/her turn to act

Nut Flush – occurs when a player hits the highest flush possible in a particular situation

Nut Flush Draw – occurs when a player is drawing to hit the nut flush

Nuts (The Nuts) – the best possible hand that a player can have in a particular situation

Odds – the mathematical probability that a player will hit one or more cards to improve or win the hand

Offsuit – when cards, usually hole cards, are not the same suit

Omaha – a version of poker in which players get four hole cards and five face-up community cards; each player must use two of his/her hole cards and three of the community cards to make the best possible five-card hand

On the Button – when a player is in the dealer position

On Tilt – when a player begins to play abnormally or wildly due to an emotional upset or to losing a big hand

One-End – a straight draw that can only be made by hitting a particular card (for example: if a player has J-Q-K-A, he can only hit a 10 to make the straight)

One-Gapper – a hand in which the two cards are one away in value (for example: 5-7—there is one gap between 5 and 7)

Open – to be the first bettor in a draw game

Open-Ender – a drawing situation where a player has four consecutive cards (example: 6-7-8-9) and needs a card from either end to complete the straight (in the example, the player would need either a 5 or a 10 to make a straight)

Open Seat – a seat at a poker table that is currently vacant but one that can be occupied by a new player

Option – if there are no raises in the first round of betting, the player who posted the big blind "has the option" to check or raise

Out, Outs – a card or cards that a player can hit to improve his hand

Out-Draw – when a player makes the winning hand by hitting a card or cards to improve it

Outrun – *see* Out-Draw

Overcall – to call a bet even after another player has called it

Overcard – a card that is higher in value than any of the community cards

Overpair – a pocket pair that is higher than the highest card on the board

Paint – face cards (Jacks, Queens, and Kings)

Pair – two of the same card

Passive – checking and calling bets, instead of betting and raising; the opposite of aggressive

Pat Hand – a hand in draw poker that is strong enough that the player does not have to draw cards

Payoff – to call on the final round of betting when a player is unsure if he has the best hand or not—if not, he is "paying off" his opponent

Pay Station – a player that frequently calls better hands and loses

Pineapple Hold'em – a poker game in which each player is dealt three hole cards and one of them must be discarded

Play Back – to raise or re-raise another player's bet

Play Behind – refers to a situation in which a player acts after someone else

Play the Board – occurs when a player's best five-card hand consists of the five community cards

Pocket Cards – *see Hole Cards*

Pocket Pair – when a player's hole cards contain a pair

Pocket Rockets – pocket Aces

Poker – a card game in which players attempt to win money by avoiding risks, making plays, bluffing, and maximizing returns on strong hands

Poker Face – not showing emotion in an effort to disguise a player's hand

Poker Room – a room specifically set aside for playing poker

Position – where a player sits in relation to the button

Position Bet – when a player bets on the basis of good position

Positional Advantage – when a player gets to see others' actions first

Post – to place a forced bet (ante or blind) into the pot

Pot – consists of all the chips that players have committed on a particular hand

Pot-Committed – occurs when there is too much money in the pot for a player to fold a hand that could be the winner

Pot-Limit – a poker game in which a player's maximum bet may not exceed the size of the pot at the time of the bet

Pot Odds – a ratio of the size of the pot to the cost of calling the bet

Pre-Flop – refers to any actions that occur before the flop is dealt

Premium Hands – pocket pairs and facecards in the hole

Price – the pot odds a player receives for hitting a draw or getting a call

Price-In – occurs when many players enter the pot and the bet is still small enough to call with weaker cards

Proposition Player, Prop – a player hired by a cardroom to help start and maintain poker games

Protect – to place an object, such as a chip or coin, on top of one's hole cards so they will not be unintentionally overturned; also, when a player bets or raises when he feels he has the best hand

Protection – occurs when a player is all-in (typically in a tournament) and a player with more chips goes all-in afterward, thus making it less likely that others will call the initial all-in bet

Put On – to figure out what hand you believe your opponent is holding

Quads – *see Four-of-a-Kind*

Rack – a tray that holds poker chips

Rags – weak cards

Ragged – a board that contains weak cards

Rail – the rim of a poker table

Rainbow – when a flop contains three cards of different suits

Raise – an action that results in a player making a bet of more chips than required to stay in the hand

Rake – a small percentage of each pot that the house collects for hosting the game

Rank – the value of each card and hand

Razz – a seven-card stud game in which the lowest hand wins

Read – to gather and sort clues from an opponent in an effort to determine the strength of his/her hand

Re-Buy – in re-buy tournaments, to buy into the tournament a second time after being eliminated but before the re-buy period expires; to buy into a cash game again

Re-Deal – a new deal after a misdeal

Re-Draw – having an extra out (for example: having a possible straight draw with a flush draw—this gives a player two ways of making a hand)

Represent – when a player acts and plays as if he has a particular hand

Re-Raise – occurs when a player raises a raise

Ring Game – *see Cash Game*

River – in hold'em, the final community card; also called "Fifth Street"

Rock – a tight player who only plays premium hands and avoids risks

Rolled-Up – in seven-card stud, when a player holds three-of-a-kind in the first three cards dealt

Royal Flush – a straight flush from ten to Ace (for example: 10-J-Q-K-A all of the same suit); the best possible hand one can have in a high poker game

"Run a Pot" – to win a hand by bluffing on more than one round of betting

Runner-Runner – a situation in which a player hits two consecutive cards (usually on the turn and river) that improve his/her hand

"Running Bad" – the term used to describe a series of hands or games in which a player has bad luck/bad cards

"Running Well," "Running Good" – the term used to describe a series of hands or games in which a player has good luck/good cards

Rush – winning many pots in a short period of time

Sandbagging – slow-playing a hand to induce a bet by another player

Satellite – a tournament in which one or more players win entry into another tournament with a larger buy-in

Scare Card – a card that is 'scary' because it could have given your opponent a better hand

Scramble – shuffling the deck by mixing the cards facedown on the table

Scoop – to win both the high- and low-pots in a split-pot game

Seat Position – in games where there is a dealer who deals all hands, seat position is the number of seats away from the dealer starting at his left and going clockwise (the player to the immediate left of the dealer is in seat 1 while the player to the dealer's right is seat 10)

Second Best – the second-highest hand in a round of poker; the best losing hand

Second Pair – a hand in which a player has a pair that consists of the second-highest card on the board and one of his hole cards

See – to call a bet

Sell – occurs when a player has a strong hand and bets less than the maximum to get one or more players to call the bet; also known as "sell a hand"

Semi-Bluff – a play in which a player makes a bet with a hand that is not made yet but could be improved on the next card (for example: if a player has a straight draw and a flush draw, he may bet or raise; if all other players fold, the player wins the pot and if there are callers, the player can still hit a number of cards to make the best hand)

Sequence – a group of consecutive cards (for example: 2-3-4-5-6)

Session – the period of time in which a poker game takes place

Set – occurs when a player has a pocket pair and a card of the same value appears on the board

"Set a Trap" – occurs when a player has a very strong hand, but plays as if he has a weak hand so his opponent is more likely to bet or call a bet

Seven-Card Stud – a poker game in which each player receives two down cards, four face-up cards, and a final down card (there are no community cards)

Seventh Street – in seven-card stud and razz, the final card that is dealt to each player (facedown)

Shark – a strong player who typically makes money off of weaker players

Shoot-Out – sometimes used to describe a tournament that has no re-buys

Short Buying – occurs in a cash game when a player has lost some of his initial chips and buys more chips from the dealer to add to his remaining stack

Short-Handed – a game in which there are fewer players at the table than the maximum allowed; usually three to five players at a table is considered a short-handed game

Short Stack – a player at a table who has a small amount of chips in comparison to most of the other players

Show – to expose one's hole cards

Show Cards – the face-up cards in stud games

Showdown – occurs when two or more players have made it through the final round of betting and they reveal their hole cards to determine who has the best hand

Shuffle – a mixing of the cards prior to the deal

Side Bet – a bet that is made that is not considered part of the pot

Side Pot – after a player has gone all-in, other players can continue to bet and raise, and the additional chips will go to a separate pot that the all-in player cannot win

Sitting Out – when a player leaves a table for a short period of time but still has chips at the table

Sixth Street – the fourth face-up card dealt in seven-card stud

Slow-Play – weakly playing the best hand to deceive other players

Slow-Roll – to slowly show one's winning hand after all the cards have come out, thus making the player with the losing hand believe he has won the pot

Small Blind – a blind bet that is required by the person to the immediate left of the dealer

Smooth Call – to simply call a bet with a strong hand, rather than raise

Snap Call – a very quick call of a bet, which usually shows that the caller has a strong hand

Snowmen – pocket eights

Soft Play – to play easier against a certain player at the table (not betting against, or raising him)

Soft Seat – a game that is desirable because most or all of the other players at the table have less skill

Solid – a tight, aware player

Speed Limit – pocket fives

Splash Around – playing much more aggressive than one should

Splash the Pot – occurs when a player aggressively tosses his/her chips into the pot, rather than neatly placing them into it

Split Pair – in stud games, having one card of the pair in the hole and the other on board

Split Pot – occurs when two or more players each receive part of the pot

Split Two Pair – in stud games, having two pair, with one of each pair in the hole and one of each pair on the board

Splitting Blinds – when everyone folds except for the blinds, the players who have posted the blinds can agree to take back their bets and end the hand without seeing a flop

Spread-Limit – a poker game in which a player can bet between a range on every round of betting (for example: in a $2-$6 spread-limit game, a player may bet anywhere from $2 to $6 on each betting round)

Squared Deck – an evenly-stacked deck that is ready to be cut or dealt

Squeeze – occurs when a player slowly looks at his hole cards

Stack – the chips a player has at the table

Stacked Deck – a deck that is intentionally set so one or more players receive strong hands; "stacking the deck" is a form of cheating and is therefore illegal

Stack-Off – to lose one's entire chip stack

Stakes – the amount of money being played for or the limits of the game

Steal – to win a pot by bluffing

Steal Position – next to last or last position in a hand (called "steal position" because the player gets to see all others' actions and can try to steal the pot if he feels all others will fold)

Steal-Raise – a raise by a player in late position to steal the pot

Steaming – *see On Tilt*

Steamrolling – re-raising to make other players fold or call two bets rather than just the initial raise

Stone-Cold Bluff – a bluff with a very weak hand that has no chance of winning the pot unless all others fold

Stop-and-Go – occurs when a player simply calls a bet and then bets or raises on the next betting round

Straddle – occurs when the player immediately to the left of the big blind posts a blind bet (usually double the amount of the big blind); the player also becomes the last person to act for the first round of betting

Straight – a hand consisting of five consecutive, unsuited cards (for example: 3-4-5-6-7)

Straight-Flush – a hand consisting of five consecutive, suited cards (for example: 3-4-5-6-7 all of hearts)

Streak – a run of winning or losing hands

String Bet – occurs when a player does not announce a bet/raise, and he/she makes more than one move of chips into the pot; whatever amount of chips was placed into the pot on the first move becomes the bet if it is a legal raise

Structure – the limits placed on the blinds, antes, bets, and raises in a game

Stud Poker – a group of poker games that use both hole cards and face-up cards in each player's hand

Suck-Out – occurs when a player with a stronger hand gets beaten by a player with a weaker hand because the remaining cards to be dealt improve the weaker hand

Suits –there are four "suits" in a typical poker deck—diamonds, hearts, spades, and clubs; five cards of the same suit make a flush

Suited – when a player's hole cards are of the same suit

Suited Connectors – two suited hole cards that can potentially make a straight or flush (for example: 8-9 of diamonds)

Table – the surface on which a game of poker is played

Table Stakes – a rule in cash games that does not allow a player to
        add more chips or money into his stack while in a hand

Tell – something that a player does or does not do that gives away
        the strength of his/her hand

Texas Hold'em – a version of poker in which each player receives
        two hole cards facedown and five community cards face-
        up; each player uses his/her two hole cards along with the
        five community cards to make his best five-card hand

Third Street – in seven-card stud games, the first up-card that is dealt
        to each player after two down-cards; the first round of
        betting takes place once third street is dealt

Three-of-a-Kind – a hand in which a player has three cards of the
        same value

Tickets – cards

Tie – a situation in which two or more players have the same hand
        and split the pot

Tight – refers to a player that does not see many flops and typically
        only plays strong hands

Tilt – *see On Tilt*

Time – a request by a player at the table when another player has
        taken substantial time to decide how to act; the player is
        typically given an additional amount of time (such as 60
        seconds) to make a decision on what to do

To Go – the amount that a player must call to remain in the hand

Tip, Toke – a monetary reward that a player gives to the dealer

Top Pair – a hand in which a player pairs the highest-value card on
        the board (for example: if a player has Q-9 in the hole

and the board is Q-10-6-4-2, he has a pair of Queens, which is the "top pair" on this particular board)

Top Set – a hand in which a player has a pair in the hole and a card of the same value is the highest-value card on the board (for example: if a player has J-J in the hole and the board is J-7-4, he has "top set")

Top Two – a hand in which a player has the top pair on the board as well as the second highest pair (for example: if a player has A-9 in the hole and the board is A-9-6-5-2, he has top pair Aces and second pair 9s, or "top two pair")

Top and Bottom – a hand in which a player has the top pair on the board as well as the bottom pair (for example: if a player has K-7 in the hole and the board is K-10-7, he has top pair Kings and bottom pair 7s)

Tournament – a poker game in which every player starts with the same number of chips and is played until one player has all of them

Treys – a pair of threes

Trips – when a player has three-of-a-kind with two of the card on the board (for example: a player holds K-7 in the hole and the board is J-7-7-2-3)

Turn – the fourth community card in a Hold'em or Omaha game

Turn Card – *see Turn*

Two-Way Hand – a hand that has possibilities of winning the high and low pots in split-pot games

Under the Gun – refers to the player who sits immediately to the left of the big blind and is first to act after the deal

Underdog – a player who is not a favorite to win a hand or game

Underpair – a pair that is lower in value than the any of the community cards (for example: if a player holds 3-3 and the board is 6-8-10, the player holds an "underpair")

Underplay – occurs when a player with a strong hand bets a small amount to increase the size of the pot

Up Card – a card in one's hand that is face-up in a stud game

Value Bet – when a player bets a hand that is not a sure winner, although over time, the bet will win more often than it loses the hand

Variance – refers to the ups and downs a player's bankroll goes through

Verbal Bet – *see Announced Bet*

Walking Sticks – pocket sevens

Wash – to shuffle the deck

Wheel – an ace-to-five straight (A-2-3-4-5); also called a "Bicycle";

Wild Card – a card that can be played as any value

Wild Game – a game played with wild cards

Wired Pair – a pocket pair

Wrap – in an Omaha game, when a player has four cards in sequence in the hole (for example: when a player holds 5-6-7-8 in the hole)

Zombie – a poker player that is difficult to read because he has no tells and shows no emotion to give away his hand

Bibliography

The Everything Poker Strategy Book by John Wenzel

www.pokernews.com/pokerterms

www.conjelco.com/pokglossary.html

For More Information

For more information about *The Complete Poker Handbook: A Guide for Players of All Skill-levels*, please visit www.CompletePokerHandbook.com

Also, your comments and suggestions are greatly appreciated; please send any comments to CompletePokerHandbook@yahoo.com